My Busy Week

Amy Davidson

ROSEN
COMMON CORE
READERS

Rosen Classroom™

New York

Published in 2013 by The Rosen Publishing Group, Inc.
29 East 21st Street, New York, NY 10010

Book Design: Michael Harmon

Photo Credits: Cover Siobhan Connally/Flickr/Getty Images; p. 5 Denise Kappa/Shutterstock.com; p. 7 Monkey Business Images/Shutterstock.com; p. 9 Vlue/Shutterstock.com; p. 11 © iStockphoto.com/Figure8Photos; p. 13 Tubol Evgeniya/Shutterstock.com; p. 15 © iStockphoto.com/CEFutcher.

ISBN: 978-1-4488-8689-0
6-pack ISBN: 978-1-4488-8690-6

Manufactured in the United States of America

CPSIA Compliance Information: Batch #WS12RC: For further information contact Rosen Publishing, New York, New York at 1-800-237-9932.

Word Count: 40

Contents

I bake a cake on Monday.

Happy
Birthday

I take a walk on Tuesday.

I go to the store
on Wednesday.

STORE

I clean my room on Thursday.

I draw a picture
on Friday.

I play with my friends
on Saturday and Sunday.

Words to Know

cake

picture

store

Index